This book is dedicated to
my four little blessings:
Ian, Aaron, Ella and Olivia.

Title ID: 6196278

ISBN-13: 978-1530963928

Bless this Mess

Written and Illustrated by:

Lori Ehlke

I'm Ian. I'm four, and Aaron is three.
Our family has added twin girls to our tree.

Ella and Olivia joined us in love,
Were healthy and happy and sent from above.

At first our two babies just ate, slept and cried.
They bounced in their bouncers, eyes opened wide.

We watched with wonder as those babies grew,
And learned how to smile, to coo and to chew.
Then Aaron and I were the most shocked of all,
When we saw our twin sisters starting to crawl.

Our cute little sisters
now go all around.

The living room's usually
where they are found.

They cover the carpet
with toy after toy.

They drive cars at each other,
squealing with joy.

Sometimes the girls will go into our room.
We rush when we hear a loud crash or big boom.

They both wriggle up and on to our beds,
Then throw sheets, dolls and pillows over their heads.

"God bless this mess," Mom and Dad like to say,
And for all of us kids, they frequently pray.

When we leave the door
of the bathroom ajar,
The little girls suddenly
appear from afar.

They pretend with make-up,
toothbrushes and more,
And we've seen them play
in the potty before!

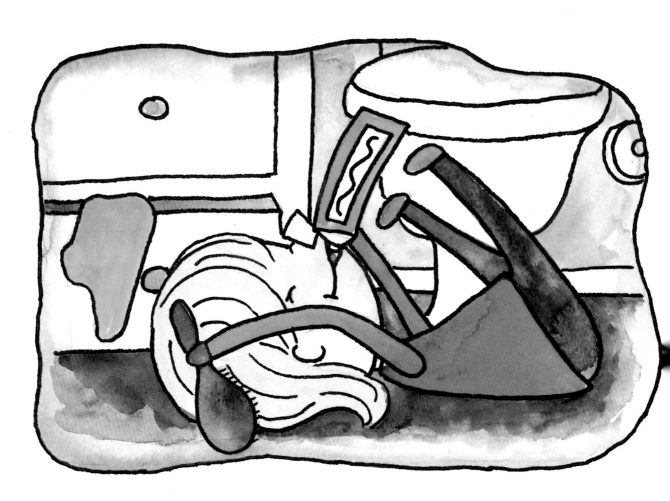

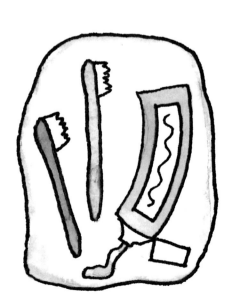

In the bathtub they splash
and throw out their toys,
Giggling and making
all sorts of noise.

They crawl to the kitchen
to see what they'll find.
The twins empty drawers,
open doors of all kinds.

Then to the dishwasher
each one will crawl,
They lick the dishes,
the big and the small.

When our twin sisters are in each high chair,
Mom gives them their food cut up with care.

Although GOOD manners Mom likes to stress,
Our sisters are better at making a mess.

"God bless this mess," Mom and Dad like to say,
And for all of us kids, they constantly pray.

Sometimes we boys
will go out to play.
The girls love to join us
any time of the day.

We boys love our sports,
our scooters and bikes.
We see that our sisters
have their own likes.

They like to throw all
of our toys to the street,
And tackle us so
they can tickle our feet.

Crawling was where
the chaos began.
But life got more crazy
when the twins learned to stand.

When Ella and Olivia
started to climb,
We found them on furniture
more than one time.
They climb onto couches,
tables and chairs.

Phones, laptops, remotes,
they think it's all theirs.

We help the twins off couches and chairs.
Our toys, food and books, we do try to share.

Having twin sisters is not always easy.
They're messy and loud and a little bit cheesy.

"God bless this mess," Mom and Dad like to say,
And for all of us kids, they persistently pray.

At seven our babies are ready for bed.
Mom puts them in jammies,
makes sure they're well fed.

The toys are all picked up and then put away.
We share songs, hugs and kisses to end their day.
We snuggle our sisters and whisper, "Goodnight".
While they're in their cribs, we turn out the light.

With the babies fast asleep in their beds,
We boys play games or watch movies instead.

Aaron and I enjoy stories and songs.
All is calm and put back
where it belongs.

Until tomorrow comes...

About the Author

Lori Ehlke is a pastor's wife and mother to two boys and twin girls. She is artistic, creative, driven and passionate and enjoys taking her four children on adventures. There are 12 sets of twins in Lori's family including her twin brothers and twin daughters.

Lori earned an Elementary Education and Spanish degree at Martin Luther College and studied Art in Florence, Italy. She has been commissioned for murals, illustrations, portraits, and more starting at the age of 16. Lori also started her own business doing art parties for adults and children.

Lori loves painting and is inspired by her children and the places that she travels. She especially likes painting old trucks because she finds the rust colors beautiful. Lori enjoys Zumba and Cardio drumming. Lori also likes to hide peanut butter M&M's in her house so she doesn't have to share them.

"Bless this Mess" is Lori's first book that she has written and illustrated and was inspired by living every day with four crazy messy children. Although they're a mess, they have been such a wonderful blessing to Lori and her husband, Brett.

41320136R00019